Coffee With C.C. (and Dami Too)

Another 7 Pattern Caffeine Inspired Knitting Collection

C.C. Almon & Dami Almon

javapurl

Hand Knit Designs Fueled by the Love of Coffee

ISBN: 978-0-9935586-1-0

Copy Editor: Katy Kidwell

Technical Editor: Rachel Brown

Models: C.C. Almon, Dami Almon, and Isaac Kidwell

Photography: Katy Kidwell

Published by JavaPurl Designs JavaPurlDesigns.com

Printed in the UK

To Katy, with love

and

To coffee, which fuels us and without which this book would never have been written

Contents

Introduction

We're the Mamma/daughter team behind JavaPurl Designs and the Geeky Girls Knit video podcast. C.C. has been designing for almost five years and with this book's patterns, Dami has released five patterns. Our pattern design inspirations range from geeky things like Doctor Who and Elementary, to colourways that demanded to be something, to the city of Edinburgh, and more.

Coffee...how can we not be inspired? After all, one of us is sure to mention on a regular basis that we need coffee in an IV, stat!

After C.C.'s first book, a collection of seven patterns inspired by coffee, we found there were a few more coffeeshop drinks that wanted to inspire us.

Our coffee tastes tend to run toward the sweeter coffee drinks, but we can appreciate all the different options. There's sure to be a coffeeshop drink to suit any situation: from babyccinos to hot chocolate (always with pink marshmallows), instant coffee to chai latte, espresso con panna to flat white, shots of espresso and everything in between.

This book is a collection of seven patterns inspired by coffeeshop drinks. Five of the patterns are for socks, each inspired by a specific drink. There is a pattern for a pair of fingerless mitts, perfect for holding your coffee in style. The final pattern is for a wrap, perfect for the cool temperatures we usually find in coffeeshops.

We hope that these caffeine inspired patterns fulfil your coffee desires whatever flavour you prefer, so grab your needles, your yarn, and a cuppa your favourite coffee and let's cast on!

Happy Knitting!
C.C. & Dami

Babyccino Socks

by Dami M. Almon

Babyccinos are a mostly-froth milky drink with no coffee that many coffeeshops offer for children.

For these socks, the rice stitch makes a bumpy textured pattern that reminds me of a babyccino's froth and is perfect for a kid (or adult) to wear.

So grab a babyccino, your yarn and your needles, and cast on your socks.
Happy Knitting!

Sizing: Baby (Toddler, Child, Adult Small, Adult Medium, Adult Large)
To fit foot circumference: 4 (5, 6, 7, 8, 9)" / 10.25 (12.75, 15.25, 17.75, 20.25, 23)cm
Recommended total foot/leg length for child sizes: 3.5 (4.5, 6)" / 9 (11.5, 15.25)cm

Gauge: 34 sts + 38 rows = 4" / 10cm in rice stitch (blocked)

Needle: US3 (3.5mm) or size needed to get gauge

Yarn: approximately 230 yds / 210 m of DK weight yarn | Sample is knit in Berry Colorful Yarnings Saturated DK Self-Striping in the Babyccino colourway

Pattern Notes:

- Pattern is written for magic loop.
- Read the pattern in its entirety before beginning so you don't miss important details.
- Instructions which are different for the 36, 44, 48, 52, and 60 st patterns will be in parentheses () separated by a comma.
- Instructions in between asterisks * * are to be repeated as notated.
- Abbreviations can be found on page 64.

Difficulty Level:

TOE-UP PATTERN:

Toe:

Cast on 10 sts per needle using Judy's Magic Cast-On.

Set-up Rnd: K10, k10tbl.

Rnd 1: *K1, M1R, k to last st on needle, M1L, k1*. Repeat on N2.
Rnd 2: Knit.

Repeat Rnds 1 and 2 until there are 14 (18, 22, 24, 26, 30) sts on each needle - 28 (36, 44, 48, 52, 60) sts total - ending with Rnd 2.

Foot:

N1 -
Rnd 1: *Ktbl, p1* to end.
Rnd 2: Purl.

N2 – Knit.

Repeat Rnds 1 and 2 until your sock measures 0.75 (1, 1.25, 1.5, 1.5, 1.75)" / 2 (2.5, 3.25, 3.75, 3.75, 4.5)cm less than the desired total foot length. On your final rnd, stop at the end of N1.

Heel:

For this section, you will be working with the sts on N2.
Row 1 (RS): K to 2 sts before end, w+t.
Row 2 (WS): P to 2 sts before end, w+t.
Row 3: K to 1 st before wrapped st, w+t.
Row 4: P to 1 st before wrapped st, w+t.
Repeat Rows 3 and 4 until 4 (4, 6, 6, 8, 8) sts remain unwrapped in the middle of N2, ending with Row 4.
Row 5: K4 (4, 6, 6, 8, 8), K4 (6, 7, 8, 8, 10) sts picking up the wrap with each st, w+t last st.
Row 6: P8 (10, 13, 14, 16, 18), p4 (6, 7, 8, 8, 10) sts picking up the wrap with each st, w+t last st.
Row 7: K8 (10, 13, 14, 16, 18), w+t.
Row 8: P4 (4, 6, 6, 8, 8), w+t.
Row 9: K to wrapped st, k wrapped st picking up the wrap with it, w+t.
Row 10: P to wrapped st, p wrapped st picking up the wrap with it, w+t.
Repeat Rows 9 and 10 until 2 wrapped sts remain on either end of N2, ending with Row 10.
Row 11: K to wrapped sts, k wrapped sts with their wraps. DO NOT TURN!
You will now have 2 wrapped sts at the beginning of N2. Begin working in the rnd, and on your next rnd (the first rnd of the leg), as you come to the wrapped sts, work the wrapped sts with their wraps.

Leg:

You will now return to working in the rnd.

N1 -
Rnd 1: *Ktbl, p1* to end.
Rnd 2: Purl.

N2 – Repeat N1 instructions.

Repeat Rnds 1 and 2 until your leg is about 0.75" / 2cm (child sizes) | 1" / 2.5cm (adult sizes) less than desired length, ending with Rnd 2.

Cuff:

Cuff Rnd: *K1tbl, p1*.
Work Cuff Rnd for 0.75" / 2cm (child sizes) | 1" / 2.5cm (adult sizes), or desired length.

Finishing:

Bind off using Jeny's Surprisingly Stretchy bind off. Weave in ends. And done! Except for the 2nd sock that is. Block. Wear. Enjoy!

CUFF-DOWN PATTERN

Cuff:

Cast on 28 (36, 44, 48, 52, 60) sts using a loose cast-on such as the German Twisted Cast-On.

Cuff Rnd: *K1tbl, p1*. Work Cuff Rnd for 0.75" / 2cm (child sizes), 1" / 2.5cm (adult sizes), or desired length.

Leg:

N1 -
Rnd 1: *Ktbl, p1* to end.
Rnd 2: Purl.

N2 – Repeat N1 instructions.

Repeat Rnds 1 and 2 until your sock measures 0.75 (1, 1.25, 1.5, 1.5, 1.75)" / 2 (2.5, 3.25, 3.75, 3.75, 4.5)cm less than the desired leg length. On your final rnd, stop at the end of N1.

Heel:

For this section, you will be working with the sts on N2.
Row 1 (RS): K to 2 sts before end, w+t.
Row 2 (WS): P to 2 sts before end, w+t.
Row 3: K to 1 st before wrapped st, w+t.
Row 4: P to 1 st before wrapped st, w+t.
Repeat Rows 3 and 4 until 4 (4, 6, 6, 8, 8) sts remain unwrapped in the middle of N2, ending with Row 4.
Row 5: K4 (4, 6, 6, 8, 8), K4 (6, 7, 8, 8, 10) sts picking up the wrap with each st, w+t last st.
Row 6: P8 (10, 13, 14, 16, 18), p4 (6, 7, 8, 8, 10) sts picking up the wrap with each st, w+t last st.
Row 7: K8 (10, 13, 14, 16, 18), w+t.
Row 8: P4 (4, 6, 6, 8, 8), w+t.
Row 9: K to wrapped st, k wrapped st picking up the wrap with it, w+t.
Row 10: P to wrapped st, p wrapped st picking up the wrap with it, w+t.
Repeat Rows 9 and 10 until 2 wrapped sts remain on either end of N2, ending with Row 10.

Row 11: K to wrapped sts, k wrapped sts with their wraps. DO NOT TURN!
You will now have 2 wrapped sts at the beginning of N2. Begin working in the rnd, and on your next rnd (the first rnd of the leg), as you come to the wrapped sts, work the wrapped sts with their wraps.

Foot:

N1 -
Rnd 1: *Ktbl, p1* to end.
Rnd 2: Purl.

N2 – Knit.

Repeat Rnds 1 and 2 until your sock measures 0.5 (0.75, 1, 1.25, 1.5, 1.75)" /1.25 (2, 2.5, 3.25, 3.75, 4.5)cm less than the desired total foot length, ending with Rnd 2.

Toe:

N1 -
Rnd 1: *K1, ssk, k to last 3 sts on needle, k2tog, k1*.
Rnd 2: Knit.

N2 – Repeat N1 instructions.

Repeat Rnds 1 and 2 until there are 10 sts on each needle – 20 sts total, ending with Rnd 2.

Finishing:

Kitchener stitch the toe. Weave in ends. And done! Except for the 2nd sock that is. Block. Wear. Enjoy!

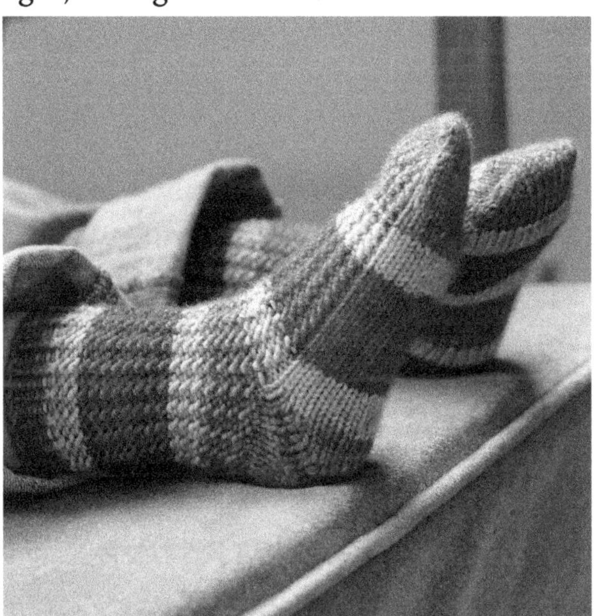

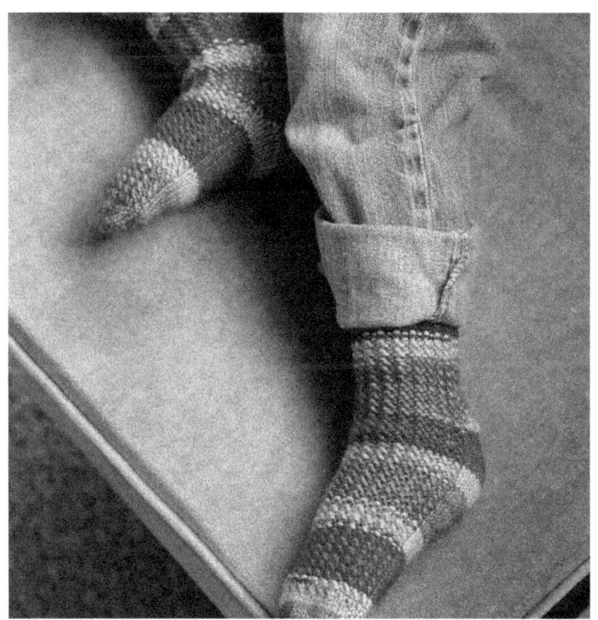

Instant Coffee Socks

by Dami M. Almon

These socks were inspired by the look and concept of instant coffee.

The look: the slipped stitch pattern reminds me of granules of instant coffee. The concept: these socks are easy and quick to make, just like instant coffee.

So grab your instant coffee, your yarn and your needles, and cast on your socks. Happy Knitting!

Sizing: Small (Medium, Large)
To fit foot circumference: 7 (7.75, 8.5)" / 17.75 (19.75, 21.5)cm

Gauge: 38 sts + 52 rows = 4" / 10cm in stitch pattern (blocked)

Needle: US3 (3.5mm) or size needed to get gauge

Yarn: approximately 273 yds / 250 m of DK weight yarn | Sample is knit in Ginger's Hand Dyed Humming DK in the My Little Pony colourway

Pattern Notes:

- Pattern is written for magic loop.
- Read the pattern in its entirety before beginning so you don't miss important details.
- Instructions which are different for the 52 and 60 st patterns will be in parentheses () separated by a comma.
- Instructions in between asterisks * * are to be repeated as notated.
- Because of how the slipped sts works within the pattern, you may need to go up a needle size, especially on the leg of the sock. Make sure and try on your sock as you go to see if you need to make any needle size modifications.
- Abbreviations can be found on page 64.

Difficulty Level:

TOE-UP PATTERN:

Toe:

Cast on 10 sts per needle using Judy's Magic Cast-On.

Set-up Rnd: K10, k10tbl.

Rnd 1: *K1, M1R, k to last st on needle, M1L, k1*. Repeat on N2.
Rnd 2: Knit.

Repeat Rnds 1 and 2 until there are 24 (26, 30) sts on each needle - 48 (52, 60) sts total - ending with Rnd 2.

Foot:

N1 -
Rnds 1 + 2: *K1, sl1* to end.
Rnds 3, 4, 7, + 8: Knit.
Rnds 5 + 6: *Sl1, k1* to end.

N2 – Knit.

Repeat Rnds 1-8 until your sock measures 1.5 (1.5, 2)" / 3.75 (3.75, 5)cm less than the desired total foot length. On your final rnd, stop at the end of N1.

Heel:

For this section, you will be working with the sts on N2.
Row 1 (RS): K to 2 sts before end, w+t.
Row 2 (WS): P to 2 sts before end, w+t.
Row 3: K to 1 st before wrapped st, w+t.
Row 4: P to 1 st before wrapped st, w+t.
Repeat Rows 3 and 4 until 6 (8, 8) sts remain unwrapped in the middle of N2, ending with Row 4.
Row 5: K6 (8, 8), K8 (8, 10) sts picking up the wrap with each st, w+t last st.
Row 6: P14 (16, 18), p8 (8, 10) sts picking up the wrap with each st, w+t last st.
Row 7: K14 (16, 18), w+t.
Row 8: P6, (8, 8), w+t.
Row 9: K to wrapped st, k wrapped st picking up the wrap with it, w+t.

Row 10: P to wrapped st, p wrapped st picking up the wrap with it, w+t.
Repeat Rows 9 and 10 until 2 wrapped sts remain on either end of N2, ending with Row 10.
Row 11: K to wrapped sts, k wrapped sts with their wraps. DO NOT TURN!

You will now have 2 wrapped sts at the beginning of N2. Begin working in the rnd, and on your next rnd (the first rnd of the leg), as you come to the wrapped sts, work the wrapped sts with their wraps.

Leg:

You will now return to working in the rnd. You need to begin with the rnd after the one you stopped with before starting the heel. Begin on the same round on N2 as you do on N1.

N1 -
Rnds 1 + 2: *K1, sl1* to end.
Rnds 3, 4, 7, + 8: Knit.
Rnds 5 + 6: *Sl1, k1* to end.

N2 – Repeat N1 instructions.

Repeat Rnds 1-8 until your sock is about 1" / 2.5cm less than desired leg length, ending with Rnd 4 or 8.

Cuff:

Cuff Rnd: *K1tbl, p1*.
Work Cuff Rnd for 1" / 2.5cm or desired length.

Finishing:

Bind off using Jeny's Surprisingly Stretchy bind off. Weave in ends. And done! Except for the 2nd sock that is! Block. Wear. Enjoy!

CUFF-DOWN PATTERN

Cuff:

Cast on 48 (52, 60) sts using a loose cast-on such as the German Twisted Cast-On.

Cuff Rnd: *K1tbl, p1*. Work Cuff Rnd for 1" / 2.5cm or desired length.

Leg:

N1 -
Rnds 1 + 2: *K1, sl1* to end.
Rnds 3, 4, 7, + 8: Knit.
Rnds 5 + 6: *Sl1, k1* to end.

N2 – Repeat N1 instructions.

Repeat Rnds 1-8 until your sock measures 1.6 (1.6, 2)" / 4 (4, 5)cm less than the desired total leg length. On your final rnd, stop at the end of N1.

Heel:

For this section, you will be working with the sts on N2.
Row 1 (RS): K to 2 sts before end, w+t.
Row 2 (WS): P to 2 sts before end, w+t.
Row 3: K to 1 st before wrapped st, w+t.
Row 4: P to 1 st before wrapped st, w+t.
Repeat Rows 3 and 4 until 6 (8, 8) sts remain unwrapped in the middle of N2, ending with Row 4.
Row 5: K6 (8, 8), K8 (8, 10) sts picking up the wrap with each st, w+t last st.
Row 6: P14 (16, 18), p8 (8, 10) sts picking up the wrap with each st, w+t last st.
Row 7: K14 (16, 18), w+t.
Row 8: P6, (8, 8), w+t.
Row 9: K to wrapped st, k wrapped st picking up the wrap with it, w+t.
Row 10: P to wrapped st, p wrapped st picking up the wrap with it, w+t.
Repeat Rows 9 and 10 until 2 wrapped sts remain on either end of N2, ending with Row 10.
Row 11: K to wrapped sts, k wrapped sts with their wraps. DO NOT TURN!

You will now have 2 wrapped sts at the beginning of N2. Begin working in the rnd, and on your next rnd (the first rnd of the leg), as you come to the wrapped sts, work the wrapped sts with their wraps.

Foot:

You will now return to working in the rnd. You need to begin with the rnd after the one you stopped with before starting the heel. N2 sts are worked in stockinette st for the entire foot.

N1 -
Rnds 1 + 2: *K1, sl1* to end.
Rnds 3, 4, 7, + 8: Knit.
Rnds 5 + 6: *Sl1, k1* to end.

N2 – Knit.

Repeat Rnds 1-8 until your sock measures 1.5 (1.5, 2)" / 3.75 (3.75, 5)cm less than the desired total foot length, ending with Rnd 4 or 8.

Toe:

N1 -
Rnd 1: *K1, ssk, k to last 3 sts on needle, k2tog, k1*
Rnd 2: Knit.

N2 – Repeat N1 instructions.

Repeat Rnds 1 and 2 until there are 10 sts on each needle - 20 sts total ending with Rnd 2.

Finishing:

Kitchener stitch the toe. Weave in ends. And done! Except for the 2nd sock that is! Block. Wear. Enjoy!

Espresso Con Panna Socks

by C.C. Almon

The Espresso Con Panna is a cuppa espresso topped with whipped cream. The strong taste of the espresso is softened by adding the whipped cream.

For these socks, I have replicated the look of an Espresso Con Panna using a textured pattern to represent the coffee's foam with the whipped cream on top.

This pattern will take on a different look depending on whether you knit with variegated yarn versus a tonal yarn versus a self-striping yarn.

So grab your Espresso Con Panna, your yarn and your needles, and cast on your socks. Happy Knitting!

Sizing: Women's Small (Medium, Large)
To fit foot circumference: 7 (8, 9)" / 17.75 (20.25, 23)cm

Gauge: 36 sts + 48 rows = 4" / 10cm in stitch pattern (blocked)

Needle: US1.5 (2.5mm) or size needed to get gauge

Yarn: approximately 462 yds / 422 m of fingering weight yarn | Sample is knit in Third Vault Yarns Librarian Sock in the Espresso Con Panna colourway

Pattern Notes:

- Pattern is written for magic loop.
- Read the pattern in its entirety before beginning so you don't miss important details.
- Instructions which are different for the 64 and 72 st patterns will be in parentheses () separated by a comma.
- The symbol Ø means there are no instructions for that size at this point, carry on to the next instruction.
- Instructions in between asterisks * * are to be repeated as notated.
- Abbreviations can be found on page 64.

Difficulty Level:

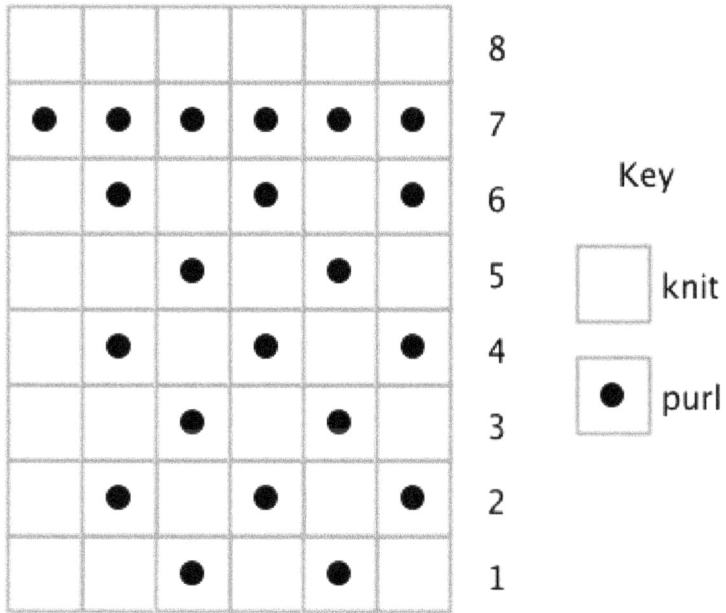

TOE-UP PATTERN:

Toe:

Cast on 8 (10, 12) sts per needle using Judy's Magic Cast-On.

Set-up Rnd: K8 (10, 12), k8tbl (10, 12).

Rnd 1: *K1, M1R, k to last st on needle, M1L, k1*. Repeat on N2.
Rnd 2: Knit.

Repeat Rnds 1 and 2 until there are 28 (32, 36) sts on each needle - 56 (64, 72) sts total - ending with Rnd 2.

Foot:

N2 sts are worked in stockinette st for the entire foot.

Chart Instructions:
N1 -
Rnds 1-6: K2 (1, Ø), work chart 4 (5, 6) times, k2 (1, Ø).
Rnd 7: Purl.
Rnd 8: Knit.
N2 – Knit.

Repeat Rnds 1-8 until your sock measures 1.5 (2, 2.25)" / 4 (5, 6)cm less than the desired total foot length. On your final rnd, stop at the end of N1.

Written Instructions:

N1 -
Rnds 1, 3, + 5: K2 (1, Ø), *k1, p1, k1, p1, k2* 4 (5, 6) times, k2 (1, Ø).
Rnds 2, 4, + 6: K2 (1, Ø), *p1, k1* 12 (15, 18) times, k2 (1, Ø).
Rnd 7: Purl.
Rnd 8: Knit.

N2 – Knit.

Repeat Rnds 1-8 until your sock measures 1.5 (2, 2.25)" / 4 (5, 6)cm less than the desired total foot length. On your final rnd, stop at the end of N1.

Heel:

For this section, you will be working with the sts on N2.
Row 1 (RS): K to 2 sts before end, w+t.
Row 2 (WS): P to 2 sts before end, w+t.
Row 3: K to 1 st before wrapped st, w+t.
Row 4: P to 1 st before wrapped st, w+t.
Repeat Rows 3 and 4 until 10 sts remain unwrapped in the middle of N2, ending with Row 4.
Row 5: K10, k8 (10, 12) sts picking up the wrap with each st, w+t last st.
Row 6: P18 (20, 22), p8 (10, 12) sts picking up the wrap with each st, w+t last st.
Row 7: K18 (20, 22), w+t.
Row 8: P10, w+t.
Row 9: K to wrapped st, k wrapped st picking up the wrap with it, w+t.
Row 10: P to wrapped st, p wrapped st picking up the wrap with it, w+t.
Repeat Rows 9 and 10 until 2 wrapped sts remain on either end of N2, ending with Row 10.
Row 11: K to wrapped sts, k wrapped sts with their wraps. DO NOT TURN!

You will now have 2 wrapped sts at the beginning of N2. Begin working in the rnd, and on your next rnd (the first rnd of the leg), as you come to the wrapped sts, work the wrapped sts with their wraps.

Leg:

You will now return to working in the rnd. You need to begin with the rnd after the one you stopped with before starting the heel. Begin on the same rnd on N2 as you do on N1.

Chart Instructions:

N1 - Work the N1 instructions from the foot for the entirety of the leg.

N2 - Work the N1 instructions from the foot for the entirety of the leg.

Continue repeating Rnds 1-8 until your sock leg is desired length minus about 1" / 2.5cm for the cuff preferably ending at the end of a repeat.

Written Instructions:

N1 - Work the N1 instructions from the foot for the entirety of the leg.

N2 - Work the N1 instructions from the foot for the entirety of the leg.

Continue repeating Rnds 1-8 until your sock leg is desired length minus about 1" / 2.5cm for the cuff preferably ending at the end of a repeat.

Cuff:

Cuff Rnd: *K1tbl, p1*.
Work Cuff Rnd for 1" / 2.5cm or desired length.

Finishing:

Bind off using Jeny's Surprisingly Stretchy bind off. Weave in ends. And done! Except for the 2nd sock that is. ;-) Block. Wear. Enjoy!

CUFF-DOWN PATTERN

Cuff:

Cast on 56 (64, 72) sts using a loose cast-on such as the German Twisted Cast-On.

Cuff Rnd: *K1tbl, p1* Work Cuff Rnd for 1" / 2.5cm or desired length.

Leg:

Chart Instructions:

N1 -
Rnds 1-6: K2 (1, Ø), work chart 4 (5, 6) times, k2 (1, Ø).
Rnd 7: Purl.
Rnd 8: Knit.

N2 – Repeat N1 instructions.
Repeat Rnds 1-8 until your sock leg measures desired leg length minus 1.5 (2, 2.25)" / 4 (5, 6)cm for the heel. On your final rnd, stop at the end of N1.

Written Instructions:

N1 -
Rnds 1, 3, + 5: K2 (1, Ø), *k1, p1, k1, p1, k2* 4 (5, 6) times, k2 (1, Ø).
Rnds 2, 4, + 6: K2 (1, Ø), *p1, k1* 12 (15, 18) times, k2 (1, Ø).
Rnd 7: Purl.
Rnd 8: Knit.

N2 - Repeat N1 instructions.
Repeat Rnds 1-8 until your sock leg measures desired leg length minus 1.5 (2, 2.25)" / 4 (5, 6)cm for the heel. On your final rnd, stop at the end of N1.

Heel:

For this section, you will be working with the sts on N2.
Row 1 (RS): K to 2 sts before end, w+t.
Row 2 (WS): P to 2 sts before end, w+t.
Row 3: K to 1 st before wrapped st, w+t.
Row 4: P to 1 st before wrapped st, w+t.
Repeat Rows 3 and 4 until 10 sts remain unwrapped in the middle of N2, ending with Row 4.
Row 5: K10, k8 (10, 12) sts picking up the wrap with each st, w+t last st.
Row 6: P18 (20, 22), p8 (10, 12) sts picking up the wrap with each st, w+t last st.
Row 7: K18 (20, 22), w+t.
Row 8: P10, w+t.
Row 9: K to wrapped st, k wrapped st picking up the wrap with it, w+t.
Row 10: P to wrapped st, p wrapped st picking up the wrap with it, w+t.
Repeat Rows 9 and 10 until 2 wrapped sts remain on either ends of N2, ending with Row 10.
Row 11: K to wrapped sts, k wrapped sts with their wraps. DO NOT TURN!

You will now have 2 wrapped sts at the beginning of N2. Begin working in the rnd, and on your next rnd (the first rnd of the foot), as you come to the wrapped sts, work the wrapped sts with their wraps.

Foot:

You will now return to working in the rnd. You need to begin with the rnd after the one you stopped with before starting the heel. N2 sts are worked in stockinette st for the entire foot.

Chart Instructions:

N1 – Work the N1 instructions from the leg.

N2 – Knit.

Continue repeating Rnds 1-8 until your sock foot measures 1.75 (2.5, 3)" /4.5 (6.5, 7.5)cm less than your desired foot length preferably ending at the end of a repeat.

Written Instructions:

N1 - Work the N1 instructions from the leg.

N2 – Knit.

Continue repeating Rnds 1-8 until your sock foot measures 1.75 (2.5, 3)" /4.5 (6.5, 7.5)cm less than your desired foot length preferably ending at the end of a repeat.

Toe:

Rnd 1:
N1 - K1, ssk, k to last 3 sts on needle, k2tog, k1.
N2 – Repeat N1 instructions.
Rnd 2: Knit.

Repeat Rnds 1 and 2 until there are 22 sts on each needle (44 sts total) ending with Rnd 2.

Repeat Rnd 1 only until there are 8 (10, 12) sts on each needle - 16 (20, 24) sts total.

Finishing:

Kitchener stitch the toe. Weave in ends. And done! Except for the 2nd sock that is. ;-) Block. Wear. Enjoy!

Chai Latte Socks

by C.C. Almon

The Chai Latte, while not technically coffee, is something that's available in most coffeeshops. It is a blend of black tea, spices, and herbs.

For these socks, I have replicated the look of the spices used in a Chai Latte using slipped stitches.

This pattern will take on a different look depending on the width of the stripes in your self-striping yarn as you alternate the pattern rows every time your yarn changes colours.

So grab your Chai Latte, your self-striping yarn, and your needles and cast on your socks. Happy Knitting!

Sizing: Women's Small (Medium, Large)
To fit foot circumference: 7 (8, 9)" / 17.75 (20.25, 23)cm

Gauge: 40 sts + 48 rows = 4" / 10cm in stitch pattern

Needle: US1.5 (2.5mm) or size needed to get gauge

Yarn: approximately 462 yds / 422 m of fingering weight yarn |
Sample is knit in Round Table Yarns Merlin in the Archimedes colourway

Pattern Notes:

- Pattern is written for magic loop.
- Read the pattern in its entirety before beginning so you don't miss important details.
- Instructions which are different for the 64 and 72 st patterns will be in parentheses () separated by a comma.
- Instructions in between asterisks * * are to be repeated as notated.
- Abbreviations can be found on page 64.

Difficulty Level:

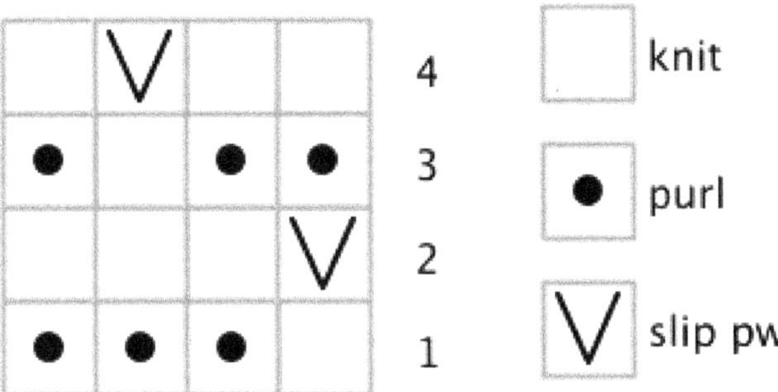

TOE-UP PATTERN:

Toe:

Cast on 8 (10, 12) sts per needle using Judy's Magic Cast-On.

Set-up Rnd: K8 (10, 12), k8tbl (10, 12).

Rnd 1: *K1, M1R, k to last st on needle, M1L, k1*. Repeat on N2.
Rnd 2: Knit.

Repeat Rnds 1 and 2 until there are 28 (32, 36) sts on each needle - 56 (64, 72) sts total - ending with Rnd 2.

Foot:

This pattern is meant to highlight self-striping yarn.The pattern has two 2 rnd repeats. Repeat Rnds 1 and 2 until your yarn changes colours. Then repeat Rnds 3 and 4 unti the next colour change. Continue alternating Rnds 1 and 2 with Rnds 3 and 4 as your yarn changes colours. N2 sts are worked in stockinette st for the entire foot.

Chart Instructions:
N1 -
All Rnds: Work chart 7 (8, 9) times.

N2 – Knit.

Repeat Rnds 1 and 2 until the colour change. Then repeat Rnds 3 and 4 until the next colour change.

Continue alternating Rnds 1 and 2 and Rnds 3 and 4. until your sock measures 1.5 (2, 2.25)" / 4 (5, 6)cm less than the desired total foot length ending with Rnd 2 or 4. On your final rnd, stop at the end of N1.

Written Instructions:

N1 -
Rnd 1: *K1, p3,* 6 (7, 8) times.
Rnd 2: *Sl1, k3* 6 (7, 8) times.
Rnd 3: *P2, k1, p1* 6 (7, 8) times.
Rnd 4: *K2, sl1, k1* 6 (7, 8) times.

N2 – Knit.

Repeat Rnds 1 and 2 until the colour change. Then repeat Rnds 3 and 4 until the next colour change.

Continue alternating Rnds 1 and 2 and Rnds 3 and 4. until your sock measures 1.5 (2, 2.25)" / 4 (5, 6)cm less than the desired total foot length. It's ok if you end without completing a full repeat. Just pay attention to this so you know what rnd to start on after the heel. On your final rnd, stop at the end of N1.

Heel:

For this section, you will be working with the sts on N2.
Row 1 (RS): K to 2 sts before end, w+t.
Row 2 (WS): P to 2 sts before end, w+t.
Row 3: K to 1 st before wrapped st, w+t.
Row 4: P to 1 st before wrapped st, w+t.
Repeat Rows 3 and 4 until 10 sts remain unwrapped in the middle of N2, ending with Row 4.
Row 5: K10, k8 (10, 12) sts picking up the wrap with each st, w+t last st.
Row 6: P18 (20, 22), p8 (10, 12) sts picking up the wrap with each st, w+t last st.
Row 7: K18 (20, 22), w+t.
Row 8: P10, w+t.
Row 9: K to wrapped st, k wrapped st picking up the wrap with it, w+t.
Row 10: P to wrapped st, p wrapped st picking up the wrap with it, w+t.
Repeat Rows 9 and 10 until 2 wrapped sts remain on either end of N2, ending with Row 10.
Row 11: K to wrapped sts, k wrapped sts with their wraps. DO NOT TURN!

You will now have 2 wrapped sts at the beginning of N2. Begin working in the rnd, and on your next rnd (the first rnd of the leg), as you come to the wrapped sts, work the wrapped sts with their wraps.

Leg:

You will now return to working in the rnd. You need to begin with Rnd 1 or 3 (start with the repeat after the one you stopped with before starting the heel). Begin on the same round on N2 as you do on N1.

Chart Instructions:

N1 - Work the N1 instructions from the foot for the entirety of the leg.

N2 - Work the N1 instructions from the foot for the entirety of the leg.

Continue repeating Rnds 1-4 until your sock leg is desired length minus about 1" / 2.5cm for the cuff ending with Rnd 2 or 4.

Written Instructions:
N1 - Work the N1 instructions from the foot for the entirety of the leg.

N2 - Work the N1 instructions from the foot for the entirety of the leg.

Continue repeating Rnds 1-4 until your sock leg is desired length minus about 1" / 2.5cm for the cuff ending with Rnd 2 or 4.

Cuff:

Cuff Rnd: *K1tbl, p1*.
Work Cuff Rnd for 1" / 2.5cm or desired length.

Finishing:

Bind off using Jeny's Surprisingly Stretchy bind off. Weave in ends. And done! Except for the 2nd sock that is. ;-) Block. Wear. Enjoy!

CUFF-DOWN PATTERN

Cuff:

Cast on 56 (64, 72) sts using a loose cast-on such as the German Twisted Cast-On.

Cuff Rnd: *K1tbl, p1* Work Cuff Rnd for 1" / 2.5cm or desired length.

Leg:

This pattern is meant to highlight self-striping yarn. The pattern has two 2 rnd repeats. Repeat Rnds 1 and 2 until your yarn changes colours. Then repeat Rnds 3 and 4 unti the next colour change. Continue alternating Rnds 1 and 2 with Rnds 3 and 4 as your yarn changes colours.

Chart Instructions:

N1 -
All Rnds: Work chart 7 (8, 9) times.

N2 –
All Rnds: Work chart 7 (8, 9) times.

Repeat Rnds 1 and 2 until the colour change. Then repeat Rnds 3 and 4 until the next colour change.

Continue alternating Rnds 1 and 2 and Rnds 3 and 4. until your sock leg measures desired leg length minus 1.5 (2, 2.25)" / 4 (5, 6)cm for the heel ending with Rnd 2 or 4. On your final rnd, stop at the end of N1.

Written Instructions:

N1 -
Rnd 1: *K1, p3,* 6 (7, 8) times.
Rnd 2: *Sl1, k3* 6 (7, 8) times.
Rnd 3: *P2, k1, p1* 6 (7, 8) times.
Rnd 4: *K2, sl1, k1* 6 (7, 8) times.

N2 - Work the N1 instructions.

Repeat Rnds 1 and 2 until the colour change. Then repeat Rnds 3 and 4 until the next colour change.

Continue alternating Rnds 1 and 2 and Rnds 3 and 4. until your sock leg measures desired leg length minus 1.5 (2, 2.25)" / 4 (5, 6)cm for the heel ending with Rnd 2 or 4. On your final rnd, stop at the end of N1.

Heel:

For this section, you will be working with the sts on N2.
Row 1 (RS): K to 2 sts before end, w+t.
Row 2 (WS): P to 2 sts before end, w+t.
Row 3: K to 1 st before wrapped st, w+t.
Row 4: P to 1 st before wrapped st, w+t.
Repeat Rows 3 and 4 until 10 sts remain unwrapped in the middle of N2, ending with Row 4.
Row 5: K10, k8 (10, 12) sts picking up the wrap with each st, w+t last st.
Row 6: P18 (20, 22), p8 (10, 12) sts picking up the wrap with each st, w+t last st.

Row 7: K18 (20, 22), w+t.
Row 8: P10, w+t.
Row 9: K to wrapped st, k wrapped st picking up the wrap with it, w+t.
Row 10: P to wrapped st, p wrapped st picking up the wrap with it, w+t.
Repeat Rows 9 and 10 until 2 wrapped sts remain on either ends of N2, ending with Row 10.
Row 11: K to wrapped sts, k wrapped sts with their wraps. DO NOT TURN!

You will now have 2 wrapped sts at the beginning of N2. Begin working in the rnd, and on your next rnd (the first rnd of the foot), as you come to the wrapped sts, work the wrapped sts with their wraps.

Foot:

You will now return to working in the rnd. You need to begin with Rnd 1 or 3 (start with the repeat after the one you stopped with before starting the heel). N2 sts are worked in stockinette st for the entire foot.

Chart Instructions:

N1 – Work the N1 instructions from the leg.

N2 – Knit.

Continue repeating Rnds 1-4 until your sock foot measures 1.75 (2.5, 3)" /4.5 (6.5, 7.5)cm less than your desired foot length ending with Rnd 2 or 4.

Written Instructions:

N1 - Work the N1 instructions from the leg.

N2 – Knit.

Continue repeating Rnds 1-4 until your sock foot measures 1.75 (2.5, 3)" /4.5 (6.5, 7.5)cm less than your desired foot length ending with Rnd 2 or 4.

Toe:

Rnd 1:
N1 - K1, ssk, k to last 3 sts on needle, k2tog, k1.
N2 – Repeat N1 instructions.
Rnd 2: Knit.

Repeat Rnds 1 and 2 until there are 22 sts on each needle (44 sts total) ending with Rnd 2.

Repeat Rnd 1 only until there are 8 (10, 12) sts on each needle - 16 (20, 24) sts total.

Finishing:

Kitchener stitch the toe. Weave in ends. And done! Except for the 2nd sock that is. ;-) Block. Wear. Enjoy!

Coffee
Shop

Flat White Wrap

by C.C. Almon

The Flat White is created by pouring steamed milk over an espresso. Because of how the milk is poured, a leaf like design is created on the top of the drink.

For this wrap, I have replicated the look of the top of the flat white using a lace design.

This wrap pattern can be modified to create a wider or skinnier wrap, a skinnier scarf, or a cowl.

So grab your Flat White, your yarn and needles, and cast on.
Happy Knitting!

Sizing: One size that is variable depending on how many repeats you complete
Sample is 16.75" / 42.5cm X 72.75" / 184.75cm

Gauge: 26 sts + 48 rows = 4" / 10cm in charted stitch pattern (blocked)

Needle: US3 (3.25mm) or size needed to get gauge

Yarn: approximately 1094 yds / 1000 m of light fingering weight yarn |
Sample is knit in Little Yellow Uke Crafts Soprano Shawl in the Flat White colourway

Pattern Notes:

- Pattern is written for knitting flat.
- Read the pattern in its entirety before beginning so you don't miss important details.
- Instructions in between asterisks * * are to be repeated as notated.
- If you'd like to make this into a skinnier scarf, cast on 17 sts (or multiples of 17 sts) less than the called for st count. Then repeat the chart/repeated instructions 1 (or the number of multiples of 17 sts) less than the pattern calls for.
- If you'd like to make this into a cowl, provisionally cast on your sts. Do not knit 6 rows. Instead start immediately with the chart/written instructions. At the end, do not knit 6 rows. Instead, graft your live sts with the provisionally cast on sts. If you'd like the cowl to be skinnier, follow the instructions above for a skinnier scarf in regards to st count.
- Abbreviations can be found on page 64.

Difficulty Level:

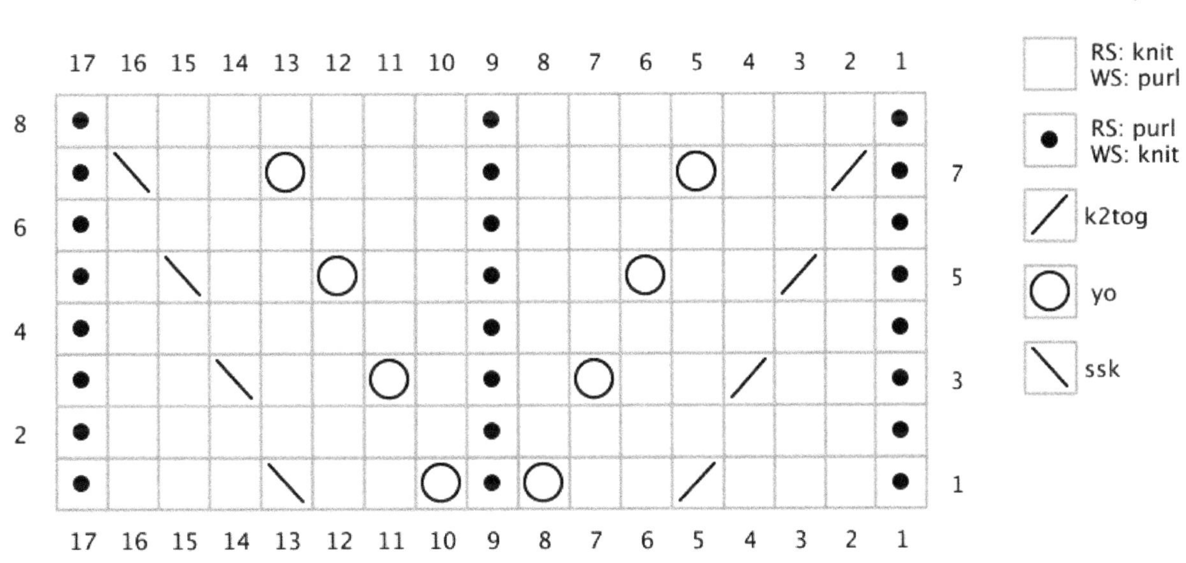

PATTERN:

Set-Up:
Cast on 125 sts.

Edging:
K all sts for 6 rows.

Body:
Chart Instructions:
All Rows: K3, work chart as written seven times, k3.
Repeat Rows 1-8 until your wrap measures desired length ending with R8.

Written Instructions:
Row 1: K3, *p1, k3, k2tog, k2, yo, p1, yo, k2, ssk, k3, p1* seven times, k3.
Rows 2, 4, 6, + 8: k3, *k1, p7, k1, p7, k1* seven times, k3.
Row 3: K3, *p1, k2, k2tog, k2, yo, k1, p1, k1, yo, k2, ssk, k2, p1* seven times, k3.
Row 5: K3, *p1, k1, k2tog, k2, yo, k2, p1, k2, yo, k2, ssk, k1, p1* seven times, k3.
Row 7: K3, *p1, k2tog, k2, yo, k3, p1, k3, yo, k2, ssk, p1* seven times, k3.
Repeat Rows 1-8 until your wrap measures desired length ending with R8.

Edging:
K all sts for 6 rows.

Finishing:
Bind off loosely.
Weave in ends. And done!
Block. Wear. Enjoy!

Hot Chocolate With Pink Marshmallows Socks

by C.C. Almon

Hot chocolate always makes me feel warm and cozy. It reminds me of love and kisses and hugs and togetherness.

For these socks, I used a cable pattern to create X's and O's. X's and O's traditionally are shorthand that means kisses and hugs.

Anyone who knows me knows that I adore the colour PINK. So of course, my hot chocolate has to have pink marshmallows in it.

So grab your Hot Chocolate with Pink Marshmallows, your yarn and your needles, and cast on your socks. Happy Knitting!

Sizing: Women's Small (Medium, Large)
To fit foot circumference: 6.25 (7, 8)" / 16 (17.75, 20.25)cm

Gauge: 51 sts + 51 rows = 4" / 10cm in stitch pattern (blocked)

Needle: US1.5 (2.5mm) or size needed to get gauge

Yarn: approximately 462 yds / 422 m of fingering weight yarn | Sample is knit in Pandia's Jewels Snug in the Cocoa With Pink Marshmallows colourway

Pattern Notes:

- Pattern is written for magic loop.
- Read the pattern in its entirety before beginning so you don't miss important details.
- Instructions which are different for the 64 and 72 st patterns will be in parentheses () separated by a comma.
- Instructions in between asterisks * * are to be repeated as notated.
- Because of the cable pattern, you may need to go up 1-2 needle sizes, especially on the leg of the sock. Make sure and try on your sock as you go to see if you need to make any needle size modifications.
- Abbreviations can be found on page 64.

Difficulty Level:

Additional abbreviations:

2/2 RC: sl2 to CN, hold in back, k2, k2 from CN

2/2 LC: sl2 to CN, hold in front, k2, k2 from CN

Key

knit

2/2 RC

2/2 LC

Chocolate Chart

Marshmallows Chart

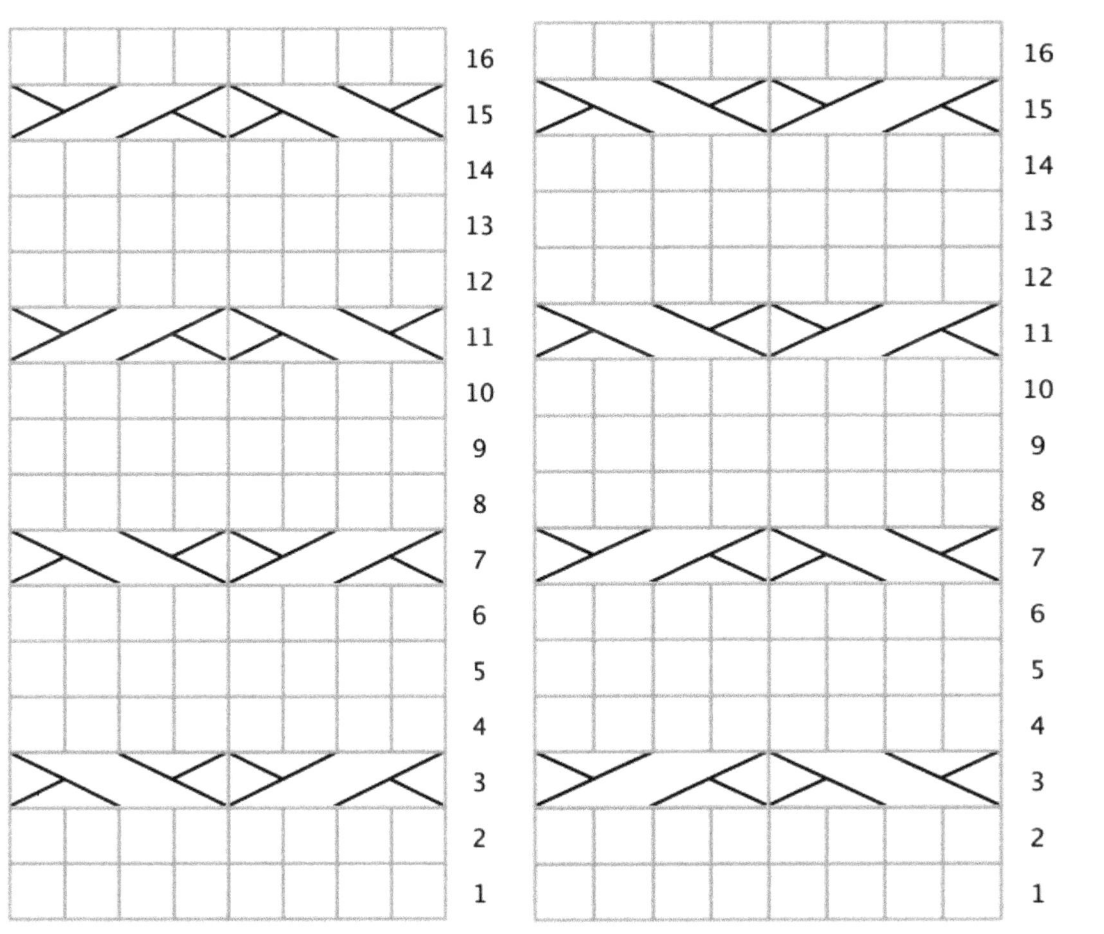

TOE-UP PATTERN:

Toe:

Cast on 8 (10, 12) sts per needle using Judy's Magic Cast-On.

Set-up Rnd: K8 (10, 12), k8tbl (10, 12).

Rnd 1: *K1, M1R, k to last st on needle, M1L, k1*. Repeat on N2.
Rnd 2: Knit.

Repeat Rnds 1 and 2 until there are 28 (32, 36) sts on each needle - 56 (64, 72) sts total - ending with Rnd 2.

Foot:

N2 sts are worked in stockinette st for the entire foot.

Chart Instructions:

N1 -
All Rnds: P1 (2, 3), work Chocolate Chart, p1 (2, 3) , work Marshmallows Chart, p1 (2, 3), work Chocolate Chart, p1 (2, 3).

N2 – Knit.

Repeat Rnds 1-16 until your sock measures 1.5 (2, 2.25)" / 4 (5, 6)cm less than the desired total foot length. It's ok if you end without completing a full repeat. Just pay attention to this so you know what rnd to start on after the heel. On your final rnd, stop at the end of N1.

Written Instructions:

N1 -
Rnds 1-2, 4-6, 8-10, 12-14, + 16: *P1 (2, 3), k8,* three times, p1 (2, 3).
Rnds 3 + 7: P1 (2, 3) 2/2 RC, 2/2 LC, p1 (2, 3), 2/2 LC, 2/2 RC, p1 (2, 3), 2/2 RC, 2/2 LC, p1 (2, 3).
Rnds 11 + 15. P1 (2, 3) 2/2 LC, 2/2 RC, p1 (2, 3), 2/2 RC, 2/2 LC, p1 (2, 3), 2/2 LC, 2/2 RC, p1 (2, 3).

N2 – Knit.

Repeat Rnds 1-16 until your sock measures 1.5 (2, 2.25)" / 4 (5, 6)cm less than the desired total foot length. It's ok if you end without completing a full repeat. Just pay attention to this so you know what rnd to start on after the heel On your final rnd, stop at the end of N1.

Heel:

For this section, you will be working with the sts on N2.
Row 1 (RS): K to 2 sts before end, w+t.
Row 2 (WS): P to 2 sts before end, w+t.
Row 3: K to 1 st before wrapped st, w+t.
Row 4: P to 1 st before wrapped st, w+t.
Repeat Rows 3 and 4 until 10 sts remain unwrapped in the middle of N2, ending with Row 4.
Row 5: K10, k8 (10, 12) sts picking up the wrap with each st, w+t last st.
Row 6: P18 (20, 22), p8 (10, 12) sts picking up the wrap with each st, w+t last st.
Row 7: K18 (20, 22), w+t.
Row 8: P10, w+t.
Row 9: K to wrapped st, k wrapped st picking up the wrap with it, w+t.
Row 10: P to wrapped st, p wrapped st picking up the wrap with it, w+t.
Repeat Rows 9 and 10 until 2 wrapped sts remain on either end of N2, ending with Row 10.
Row 11: K to wrapped sts, k wrapped sts with their wraps. DO NOT TURN!

You will now have 2 wrapped sts at the beginning of N2. Begin working in the rnd, and on your next rnd (the first rnd of the leg), as you come to the wrapped sts, work the wrapped sts with their wraps.

Leg:

You will now return to working in the rnd. You need to begin with the rnd after the one you stopped with before starting the heel. Begin on the same round on N2 as you do on N1.

Chart Instructions:
N1 - Work the N1 instructions from the foot.

N2 -
All Rnds: P1 (2, 3), work Marshmallows Chart, p1 (2, 3) , work Chocolate Chart, p1 (2, 3), work Marshmallows Chart, p1 (2, 3).

Continue repeating Rnds 1-16 until your sock leg is desired length minus about 1" / 2.5cm for the cuff ending with any Rnd.

Written Instructions:
N1 - Work the N1 instructions from the foot.

N2 -
Rnds 1-2, 4-6, 8-10, 12-14, + 16: *P1 (2, 3), k8,* three times, p1 (2, 3).
Rnds 3 + 7: P1 (2, 3) 2/2 LC, 2/2 RC, p1 (2, 3), 2/2 RC, 2/2 LC, p1 (2, 3), 2/2 LC, 2/2 RC, p1 (2, 3).
Rnds 11 + 15: P1 (2, 3) 2/2 RC, 2/2 LC, p1 (2, 3), 2/2 LC, 2/2 RC, p1 (2, 3), 2/2 RC, 2/2 LC, p1 (2, 3).

Continue repeating Rnds 1-16 until your sock leg is desired length minus about 1" / 2.5cm for the cuff ending with any Rnd.

Cuff:

Cuff Rnd: *K1tbl, p1*.
Work Cuff Rnd for 1" / 2.5cm or desired length.

Finishing:

Bind off using Jeny's Surprisingly Stretchy bind off. Weave in ends. And done! Except for the 2nd sock that is. ;-) Block. Wear. Enjoy!

CUFF-DOWN PATTERN

Cuff:

Cast on 56 (64, 72) sts using a loose cast-on such as the German Twisted Cast-On.

Cuff Rnd: *K1tbl, p1* Work Cuff Rnd for 1" / 2.5cm or desired length.

Leg:

Chart Instructions:

N1 -
All Rnds: P1 (2, 3), work Chocolate Chart, p1 (2, 3) , work Marshmallows Chart, p1 (2, 3), work Chocolate Chart, p1 (2, 3).

N2 -
All Rnds: P1 (2, 3), work Marshmallows Chart, p1 (2, 3) , work Chocolate Chart, p1 (2, 3), work Marshmallows Chart, p1 (2, 3).

Continue repeating Rnds 1-16 until your sock leg measures desired leg length minus 1.5 (2, 2.25)" / 4 (5, 6)cm for the heel. (It's ok if you end without completing a full repeat. Just pay attention to this so you know what rnd to start on after the heel.) On your final rnd, stop at the end of N1.

Written Instructions:

N1 -
Rnds 1-2, 4-6, 8-10, 12-14, + 16: *P1 (2, 3), k8,* three times, p1 (2, 3).
Rnds 3 + 7: P1 (2, 3) 2/2 RC, 2/2 LC, p1 (2, 3), 2/2 LC, 2/2 RC, p1 (2, 3), 2/2 RC, 2/2 LC, p1 (2, 3).
Rnds 11 + 15: P1 (2, 3) 2/2 LC, 2/2 RC, p1 (2, 3), 2/2 RC, 2/2 LC, p1 (2, 3), 2/2 LC, 2/2 RC, p1 (2, 3).

N2 -
Rnds 1-2, 4-6, 8-10, 12-14, + 16: *P1 (2, 3), k8,* three times, p1 (2, 3).
Rnds 3 + 7: P1 (2, 3) 2/2 LC, 2/2 RC, p1 (2, 3), 2/2 RC, 2/2 LC, p1 (2, 3), 2/2 LC, 2/2 RC, p1 (2, 3).
Rnds 11 + 15: P1 (2, 3) 2/2 RC, 2/2 LC, p1 (2, 3), 2/2 LC, 2/2 RC, p1 (2, 3), 2/2 RC, 2/2 LC, p1 (2, 3).

Continue repeating Rnds 1-16 until your sock leg measures desired leg length minus 1.5 (2, 2.25)" / 4 (5, 6)cm for the heel. (It's ok if you end without completing a full repeat. Just pay attention to this so you know what rnd to start on after the heel.) On your final rnd, stop at the end of N1.

Heel:

For this section, you will be working with the sts on N2.
Row 1 (RS): K to 2 sts before end, w+t.
Row 2 (WS): P to 2 sts before end, w+t.
Row 3: K to 1 st before wrapped st, w+t.
Row 4: P to 1 st before wrapped st, w+t.
Repeat Rows 3 and 4 until 10 sts remain unwrapped in the middle of N2, ending with Row 4.
Row 5: K10, k8 (10, 12) sts picking up the wrap with each st, w+t last st.
Row 6: P18 (20, 22), p8 (10, 12) sts picking up the wrap with each st, w+t last st.
Row 7: K18 (20, 22), w+t.
Row 8: P10, w+t.
Row 9: K to wrapped st, k wrapped st picking up the wrap with it, w+t.
Row 10: P to wrapped st, p wrapped st picking up the wrap with it, w+t.
Repeat Rows 9 and 10 until 2 wrapped sts remain on either ends of N2, ending with Row 10.
Row 11: K to wrapped sts, k wrapped sts with their wraps. DO NOT TURN!

You will now have 2 wrapped sts at the beginning of N2. Begin working in the rnd, and on your next rnd (the first rnd of the foot), as you come to the wrapped sts, work the wrapped sts with their wraps.

Foot:

You will now return to working in the rnd. You need to begin with the rnd after the one you stopped with before starting the heel. N2 sts are worked in stockinette st for the entire foot.

Chart Instructions:

N1 – Work the N1 instructions from the leg.

N2 – Knit.

Continue repeating Rnds 1-16 until your sock measures 1.75 (2.5, 3)" / 4.5 (6.5,7.5)cm less than your desired foot length, ending with any Rnd.

Written Instructions:

N1 - Work the N1 instructions from the leg.

N2 – Knit.

Continue repeating Rnds 1-16 until your sock measures 1.75 (2.5, 3)" /4.5 (6.5, 7.5)cm less than your desired foot length, ending with any Rnd.

Toe:

Rnd 1:
N1 - K1, ssk, k to last 3 sts on needle, k2tog, k1.
N2 – Repeat N1 instructions.
Rnd 2: Knit.

Repeat Rnds 1 and 2 until there are 22 sts on each needle (44 sts total) ending with Rnd 2.

Repeat Rnd 1 only until there are 8 (10, 12) sts on each needle - 16 (20, 24) sts total.

Finishing:

Kitchener stitch the toe. Weave in ends. And done! Except for the 2nd sock that is. ;-) Block. Wear. Enjoy!

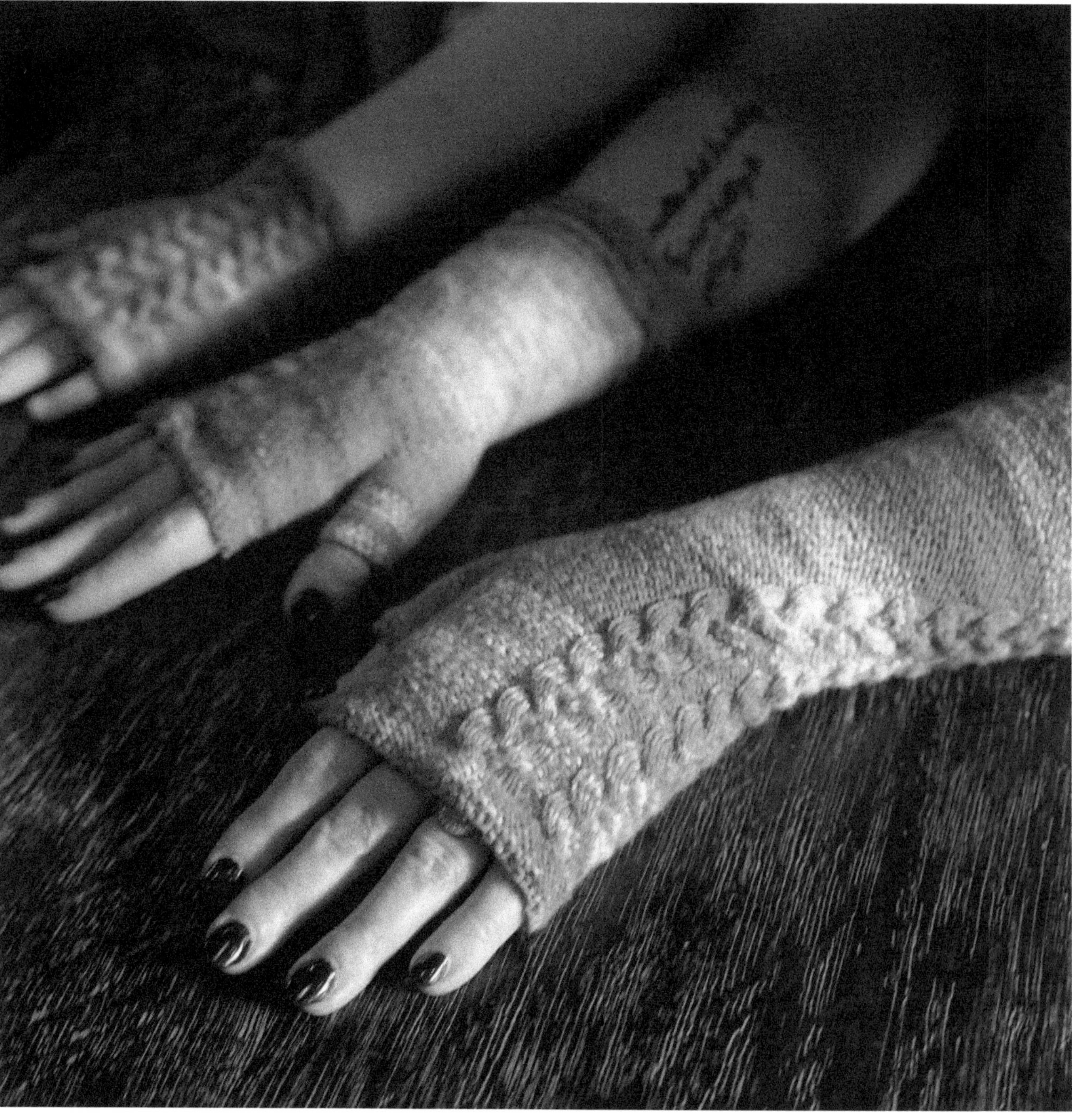

1 Shot, 2 Shots, 3 Shots Fingerless Mitts

by C.C. Almon

When I thought of designing a pair of fingerless mitts, espresso shots came to mind. Espresso shots are created by forcing almost boiling water through finely ground coffee beans.

For these mitts, the cable pattern is a braid of three strands repeated three times around the mitts. There are 3 length options appropriately named 1 Shot, 2 Shots, or 3 Shots.

So grab a shot (or two or three) of espresso, your yarn and your needles, and cast on your mitts. Happy Knitting!

Sizing: Adult Small (Medium, Large)
Hand circumference: 7 (7.5, 8)" / 17.75 (19, 20)cm
Length of mitts: 1 shot is wrist length, 2 shots is mid-forearm length, and 3 shots is just below the elbow length

Gauge: 33 sts = 2.25" / 5.75 cm in the cable pattern worked 3 times across and 24 rows = 2.5" / 6.25 cm repeated 3 times

Needle: US2 (2.75mm) or size needed to get gauge

Yarn: approximately 437 yds / 400 m of fingering weight yarn | Sample is knit in Rusty Ferret Yarns RF Quadrupole in the Steampunk colourway

Pattern Notes:

- Pattern is written for magic loop.
- Read the pattern in its entirety before beginning so you don't miss important details.
- Instructions which are different for the M and L sizes will be in parentheses () separated by a comma.
- Instructions in between asterisks * * are to be repeated as notated.
- You will need three stitch markers designated mA, mB, and mC.
- Abbreviations can be found on page 64.
- The symbol Ø means there are no instructions for that size at this point, carry on to the next instruction.

Difficulty Level:

Additional abbreviations:

M: marker

M1LP: make 1 left purl (pick up strand of yarn between 2 sts from front to back and purl through the back of lifted strand) [1 st increased]

M1RP: make 1 right purl (pick up strand of yarn between 2 sts from back to front and purl through the front of lifted strand) [1 st increased]

p2tog: purl 2 sts together [1 st decreased]

pm: place marker

sM: slip marker

ssp: sl2 individually kw from left needle to right needle, transfer both sts back to the left needle pw, purl these two sts together through the back loop. [1 st decreased]

3/3 LC: sl3 to CN, hold in front, k3, k3 from CN

3/3 RC: sl3 to CN, hold in back, k3, k3 from CN

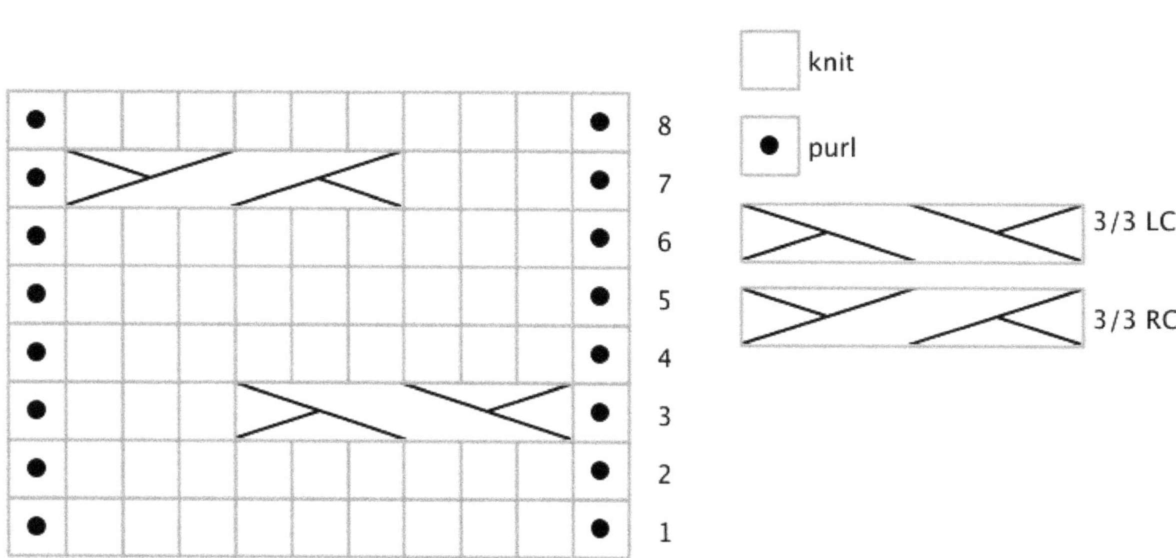

PATTERN:

Cast-On:

First, you need to decide what length of mitt you want to knit. 1 shot is wrist length, 2 shots is mid-forearm length, and 3 shots is just below the elbow length.

For 1 shot length, cast on 55 (59, 65) sts.
For 2 shots length, cast on 69 (75, 79) sts.
For 3 shots length, cast on 85 (89, 95) sts.

All sizes/lengths:
Join in the round. K 1 rnd. P 5 rnds.

Wrist:

The 2 shots and 3 shots lengths require decreases to get your stitch count down to the appropriate size for your hand circumference. For both lengths, you will decrease every 6 rnds as follows: ssp, work to last 2 sts, p2tog. Repeat this decrease rnd every 6th rnd. Continue repeating these decreases while following the pattern below until you have Ø (59, 65) sts on your needle.

Chart Instructions:
Set-up rnd:
1 shot: P11 (13, 16), pmA, work chart three times, pmB, p11 (13, 16).
2 shots: P18 (21, 23), pmA, work chart three times, pmB, p18 (21, 23).
3 shots: P26 (28, 31), pmA, work chart three times, pmB, p26 (28, 31).

All rnds: P to mA, smA, work chart three times, smB, p to end of rnd.

Continue repeating Rnds 1-8 (while working decreases for the 2 and 3 shots lengths) until your mitt measures 2" / 5cm (1 shot), 5" / 12.75 cm (2 shots), or 8" / 20.25 cm (3 shots) from cast on edge.

Written Instructions:
Set-up rnd:
1 shot: P11 (13, 16), pmA, *p1, k9, p1* three times, pmB, p11 (13, 16).
2 shots: P18 (21, 23), pmA, *p1, k9, p1* three times, pmB, p18 (21, 23).
3 shots: P26 (28, 31), pmA, *p1, k9, p1* three times, pmB, p26 (28, 31).

There are 2 sets of instructions in this section. You will follow the Glass Instructions for every rnd while working Rnds 1-8 of the Shot Instructions in order.

For the first repeat of Rnds 1-8 only, begin with Rnd 2 of the Shot Instructions (because you worked Rnd 1 in the Set-up rnd).

Glass Instructions:
All rnds: P to mA, smA, work Shot Instructions, smB, p to end of rnd.

Shot Instructions:
Rnds 1, 2, 4-6, and 8: *P1, k9, p1* three times.
Rnd 3: *P1, 3/3 LC, k3, p1* three times.
Rnd 7: *P1, k3, 3/3 RC, p1* three times

Continue repeating Rnds 1-8 (while working decreases for the 2 and 3 shots lengths) until your mitt measures 2" / 5cm (1 shot), 5" / 12.75 cm (2 shots), or 8" / 20.25 cm (3 shots) from cast on edge.

Left Thumb Gusset:

Chart Instructions:

You need to begin with the rnd after the one you stopped with in the Wrist section. Continue working the chart while following the gusset instructions below.

Set-Up rnd: M1RP, p5, M1LP, pmC, p to mA, smA, work chart three times, smB, p11 (13, 16).

Rnds A and B: P to mA, smA, work chart three times, smB, p11 (13, 16).
Rnd C: M1RP, p to mC, smC, M1LP, p to mA, smA, work chart three times, smB, p11 (13, 16).

Work Rnds A-C 7 (7, 8) times total. You'll have 21 (21, 23) sts from start of rnd to mC and 50 (54, 60) sts from mC to end of rnd.

Sl21 (21, 23) sts from start of rnd to mC on waste yarn. Remove mC, p1, *M1RP, p1* five times and return to original instructions of p to mA, smA, work chart three times, smB, p to end of rnd.

Written Instructions:

You need to begin with the rnd after the one you stopped with in the Wrist section Shot Instructions. Continue working the Shot Instructions while following the gusset instructions below.

Set-Up rnd: M1RP, p5, M1LP, pmC, p to mA, smA, work Shot Instructions, smB, p11 (13, 16).

Rnds A and B: P to mA, smA, work Shot Instructions, smB, p11 (13, 16).
Rnd C: M1RP, p to mC, smC, M1LP, p to mA, smA, work Shot Instructions, smB, p11 (13, 16).

Work Rnds A-C 7 (7, 8) times total. You'll have 21 (21, 23) sts from start of rnd to mC and 50 (54, 60) sts from mC to end of rnd.

Sl21 (21, 23) sts from start of rnd to mC to waste yarn. Remove mC, p1, *M1RP, p1* five times and return to original instructions of p to mA, smA, work chart three times, smB, p to end of rnd.

Right Thumb Gusset:

Chart Instructions:

You need to begin with the rnd after the one you stopped with in the Wrist section. Continue working the chart while following the gusset instructions below.

Set-Up rnd: P to mA, smA, work chart three times, smB, p to last 5 sts, PmC, M1RP, p5, M1LP.

Rnds A and B: P to mA, smA, work chart three times, smB, p to mC, smC, p to end of rnd.
Rnd C: P to mA, smA, work chart three times, smB, p to mC, smC, M1Rp, p to end of rnd, M1LP.

Work Rnds A-C 7 (7, 8) times total. You'll have 50 (54, 60) sts from start of rnd to mC and 21 (21, 23) sts from mC to end of rnd.

P to mA, smA, work chart three times, smB, p to 5 (5, 6) sts before mC, p1, *M1RP, p1* five times, remove mC, sl21 (21, 23) sts from mC to end of rnd to waste yarn.

Written Instructions:

You need to begin with the rnd after the one you stopped with in the Wrist section Shot Instructions. Continue working the Shot Instructions while following the gusset instructions below.

Set-Up rnd: P to mA, smA, work Shot Instructions, smB, p to last 5 sts, PmC, M1RP, p5, M1LP.

Rnds A and B: P to mA, smA, work Shot Instructions, smB, p to mC, smC, p to end of rnd.
Rnd C: P to mA, smA, work Shot Instructions, smB, p to mC, smC, M1Rp, p to end of rnd, M1LP.

Work Rnds A-C 7 (7, 8) times total. You'll have 50 (54, 60) sts from start of rnd to mC and 21 (21, 23) sts from mC to end of rnd.

P to mA, smA, work Shot Instructions, smB, p to 5 (5, 6) sts before mC, p1, *M1RP, p1* five times, remove mC, sl21 (21, 23) sts from mC to end of rnd to waste yarn.

Hand:

Chart Instructions:

You need to begin with the chart rnd after the one you stopped with in the Gusset section. Continue working the chart while following the hand instructions below.
All rnds: P to mA, smA, work chart three times, smB, p to end of rnd.

Continue repeating Rnds 1-8 until your mitt measures 2 (2.25, 2.5)" / 5 (5.75, 6.25)cm from the increase rnd in the Gusset section ending with Rnds 4 or 8.

P 5 rnds. K 1 rnd. BO loosely.

Written Instructions:

You need to begin with the rnd after the one you stopped with in the Gusset section Shot Instructions. Continue working the Shot Instructions while following the hand Glass Instructions below.

Glass Instructions:

All rnds: P to mA, smA, work Shot Instructions, smB, p to end of rnd.
Continue repeating Rnds 1-8 until your mitt measures 2 (2.25, 2.5)" / 5 (5.75, 6.25)cm from the increase rnd in the Gusset section ending with Rnds 4 or 8.

P 5 rnds. K 1 rnd. BO loosely.

Thumb:

Place sts from waste yarn onto needle. Join in the round. P21 (21, 23) and then pick up 2 sts from the body of mitt for a total of 23 (23, 25) sts. P all to 1 (1.25, 1.5)" / 2.5 (3.25, 3.75)cm. K 1 rnd. BO loosely.

Finishing:

Weave in ends. And done! Except for the 2nd mitt that is. ;-) Block. Wear. Enjoy!

Abbreviations

CN cable needle

k knit

k2tog knit 2 sts together [1 st decreased]

ktbl knit through the back loop

kw knitwise

M1L make 1 left (pick up strand of yarn between 2 sts from front to back and knit through the back of lifted strand) [1 st increased]

M1R make 1 right (pick up strand of yarn between 2 sts from back to front and knit through the front of lifted strand) [1 st increased]

N needle

p purl

pw purlwise

Rnd Round

RS right side

sl slip 1 st pw

ssk sl2 kw 1 at a time, insert the left needle into the fronts of the 2 sts and knit together [1 st decreased]

st(s) stitch(es)

w+t (wrap and turn) into a knit st Insert right needle into the st below the st to be wrapped from right to left, lift that st and place it onto the left needle. Knit into the st just placed onto the left needle, then move the st being wrapped from the right to the left needle; you'll now have 2 sts coming out of the same st on the left needle. Turn to work the other direction - the

	2 sts coming out of the single st count as 1 st when counting sts. When you are ready to knit the st with the wrap, knit the 2 sts of the wrapped st together.
w+t (wrap and turn) into a purl st	Slip the st to be wrapped pw from the left needle to the right needle, and insert left needle into the st below the st to be wrapped from left to right. Lift the st and place it onto the left needle, then purl into the st you just placed onto the left needle; you'll now have 2 sts coming out of the same st on your right needle. Slip both sts pw to the left needle, and turn to work the other direction - the 2 sts coming out of the single st count as 1 st when counting sts. When you are ready to purl the st with the wrap, purl the 2 sts that are coming out of the single st together.
WS	wrong side
wyif	with yarn in front
yo	yarnover [1 st increased]

Difficulty Level

It seemed appropriate for the difficulty level for the patterns in this book to be expressed using a coffee strength scale.

Light　　Medium　　Strong

For special technique tutorials, visit our website

JavaPurlDesigns.com

Acknowledgements

From C.C.

To the Hubs, Russ, thank you times infinity for your never-ending support, encouragement, and love. Thank you for walking this journey with me. I love you the mostest-ostest-ostest!

To my daughter, Dami, thank you for your support, encouragement, and love. Thank you for co-hosting the podcast with me every single week, for being my sample knitter, and for being the model for so many of my photoshoots. You're my Lorelai Gilmore! I love you!

To my Great-Grandmother, Opal Cady, my Nana, Bertha Hobson, and my Momma, Beckey Wolfe, who crafted when I was a child and encouraged me to craft too.

To my bestie, Katy Kidwell, thank you for copy editing my book, taking the photos for these patterns, and for always being so excited about what I'm knitting now. You are the best friend I could ever hope for. I am so grateful for that random social media connection which brought our families together. Love you sweetie!

To my BFF (best fibre friend), Jill McCullough, thank you for your support and friendship. Our daily Voxer chats are one of the highlights of my day. I am so grateful for you. Love you tons!

From Dami

To my parents, both of whom inspire me on a daily basis, and to all the other creatives whom I've had the pleasure of admiring, whose work fills this grey world with every imaginable colour.

From Us

To the amazing yarn dyers who dyed the yarn for this book, Michelle Berry of Berry Colorful Yarnings, Jessica James of Ginger Twist Studio, Lola Johnson of Third Vault Yarns, Karen Robinson of Round Table Yarns, Zena Perry-Hartle of Little Yellow Uke Crafts, Julia Wardell of Pandia's Jewels, and Leona-Jayne Kelly of Rusty Ferret Yarns, thank you for your creative colour genius that inspires us on a daily basis.

To our test knitters, Ann Bostic, Rhonda Duell, Tracy Gilman, Andrea Jones, Kimberly Napier, GeorgeAnne Plaza, Kirsi Salmi, and Ashleah Younker, thank you for finding our mistakes, advising us, and taking your time to knit our patterns.

To Rachel Brown of Porpoise Fur, thank you for being an amazing tech editor. You've taken our jumbled words and made them flow smoothly.

To the multitude of podcasters in the fibre world, thanks for keeping us company as we work. Special shout-outs to Jasmin and Gigi of The Knitmore Girls, Jilly of The Knitting Broomstick, Dianne of Suburban Stitcher, Rachel and Alli of Yarn in the City, and Tara of Explore Your Enthusiasm. Thank you for your support and friendship!

To Starbucks, Costa, 200° Coffee, and York's Espresso Bar for allowing us to shoot the photos for this book in their spaces.

To Sam Boggia of KnitRunDig Project Bags, thanks for creating bags that we're thrilled to put our projects into. You are such a kind friend and we're thankful for you!

To the world of knitting designers, your creativity and brilliant patterns inspire us.

To the members of the Starship, thank you for celebrating our joys, offering support for our problems, and coming up with creative ideas to better our business.

To the viewers of the Geeky Girls Knit Podcast, thank you for journeying with us through our random, crazy, rambling weekly show. You are the best viewers podcasters could ever hope for.

To each person who has knit one or more of our patterns, thank you for taking our creativity and making it your own.

About C.C. & Dami

Hiya! I'm C.C. Almon. I'm half of the JavaPurl Designs / Geeky Girls Knit Podcast team. A little about me: I've been married for 19+ years to the love of my life Russ (aka The Hubs). I have a beautiful 17+ year old daughter Dami. We live in Edinburgh, Scotland where the Hubs is studying for his Ph.D.

I'm a self-taught knitter (began in 2005) and can crochet just enough to be dangerous. I began designing knitting patterns in 2012.

I'm addicted to coffee, the Gilmore Girls, Doctor Who, the colour pink, lots of geeky things, and knitting!

Hi, I'm Dami Almon!

I'm the other half of JavaPurl Designs and the Geeky Girls Knit podcast. I was taught to knit by my mom in 2007, and in recent years my love for it has only grown. I began designing patterns in 2016.

I'm in love with classic lit, Broadway (Great Comet! Hamilton!), a slew of geeky TV shows, and somewhat loosely consider myself an artist and writer.

Find US Online

Website: JavaPurlDesigns.com
Email: grande@JavaPurlDesigns.com
Ravelry: JavaPurl | damisdoodles
Ravelry Group: JavaPurl Designs

Since 2012, we have co-hosted the weekly video podcast, Geeky Girls Knit.
Website: GeekyGirlsKnit.com
Ravelry Group: Geeky Girls Knit Podcast

Lightning Source UK Ltd.
Milton Keynes UK
UKHW05f0934080618
323884UK00006B/103/P

9 780993 558610